Honey Hunters

Written by Bridie Dickson

Illustrated by Meredith Thomas

Flying Start
to Literacy®

Contents

Prologue

The Hadza people of Tanzania, in Africa, are one of the last remaining hunter-gatherer societies in the world. They are nomadic – they have no permanent homes, and they move from place to place to hunt and gather their food. They hunt animals such as giraffes, zebras, baboons and birds, and they gather fruits, berries and nuts.

A big part of their diet is wild honey that they collect from beehives. The problem is, these beehives are often hidden in the cavities of tall trees. But the wild honeyguide bird helps the hunters find the beehives. When the Hadza want to find a beehive, they make a specialised call and the honeyguide bird responds. It whistles and chatters back with the honey hunters following, until it reaches a beehive.

The honey hunters then open up the beehive and collect the honey from inside. Meanwhile, the honeyguide bird waits around for any scraps.

This is a fascinating partnership in which both the people and the birds benefit. It is thought to be the only mutualistic partnership between humans and wild animals in the world today.

Chapter 1
Koyobe

Twit twit tah-weee. Twit twit tah-weee.

The familiar whistle woke Koyobe. He groaned inwardly as he shifted into a more comfortable position. He'd been enjoying his midday nap in the shade.

"Koyobe!" His father's voice stopped him from dozing off. "The honeyguide is here. Let's go honey hunting."

Koyobe sat up and yawned. "Do I have to go?"

"Come! Watch and learn. You might need this information one day," said Koyobe's father, Musa.

Koyobe didn't feel like going honey hunting. But he couldn't disappoint his father, who was always telling him about the importance of their culture.

Koyobe reluctantly grabbed his axe and headed over to Musa. They shielded their eyes from the sun as they scanned the sky.

"There he is," said Musa, pointing. They followed the small bird as it whistled and chattered, and flew from tree to tree.

Musa answered the bird using the familiar honey-hunting whistle.

Koyobe didn't join in. He was thinking about the visitors who were coming all the way from America and arriving at their camp in a few days. He wondered what they might be like. He couldn't wait to find out!

Koyobe watched as the bird stopped in the branches of an acacia tree. He scurried up the tree and peeled back some bark to reveal the beehive.

"Good work, Koyobe!"

Musa's praise made Koyobe feel warm inside, and then immediately guilty that he'd been so negative about hunting honey with his father.

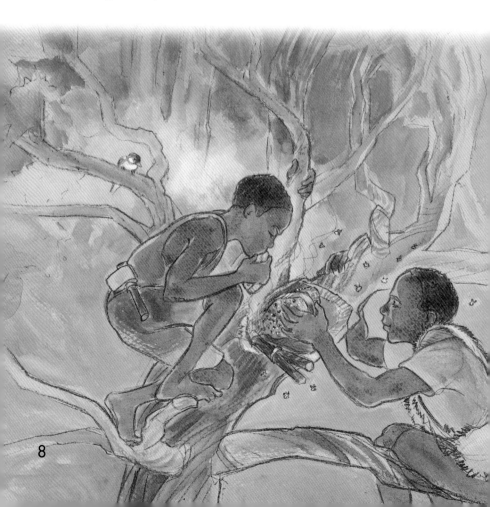

Musa climbed up the tree with a smoking fire stick in his hand, and he poked the stick into the beehive to quieten the bees. Once the bees were calm, Koyobe sliced the hive wide open with his axe.

Together, Musa and Koyobe pulled large pieces of bright golden honeycomb out of the hive and dropped them onto the ground below.

"Our visitors will love this!" Musa said. He was pleased with the harvest and he scooped it up into a bucket.

"I can't wait to meet them," said Koyobe. "And I can't wait to see Tembo again." Tembo was Koyobe's cousin. He lived in the big town, where he worked as a tour guide.

"He's been showing people all around Tanzania," Musa said. "And he'll be depending on us to show the visitors our Hadza ways." Musa was very proud of their traditions.

"They'll be impressed." Koyobe was already planning what he'd show them.

Chapter 2

Jemma

The truck bumped and swerved as it navigated the pot-holed dirt road. Jemma held on tightly to the door handle and concentrated on keeping her balance. Every time she looked out the window, the scenery was the same – spiky grasses and shrubs, short trees dotting the earth here and there, and smooth brown rocks.

Jemma glanced at the front seat, where her mum was asking Tembo, their tour guide, a million questions. Jemma smiled to herself. She knew it was pretty cool to have an award-winning journalist as her mother.

"Not long now, Jem!" Jemma's mum grinned as she looked back over her shoulder.

Jemma tried to match her mum's smile, but she wasn't feeling that happy about this so-called holiday. Her mind drifted back to the day her mother had told her about their trip . . .

"How would you like to come with me on my next work trip?" Jemma's mum asked excitedly.

"Yes! Of course!" Jemma gasped. Her mind raced – would they go to the beach? A theme park? Maybe they'd go to Europe and visit an art gallery?

"We're off to Tanzania. In Africa," Jemma's mum announced. "And we're even staying a night with the nomadic Hadza people. I'm writing an article about them."

"Oh." Jemma tried to hide her disappointment. "Africa?" She wasn't expecting that.

Jemma's mum was away a lot, so Jemma was glad she could spend this time with her. She put a big smile on her face and said, "It'll be fun!"

But now, in the heat and the dust and the bumps, she wasn't too sure!

At long last, they finally stopped.

"We're here," Tembo grinned. "These are my people!" And he jumped out of the truck with Jemma's mum close behind.

Jemma looked out the window. *Where do they sleep? What kind of food do they eat? What do they do for fun in this hot, dusty place?*

Jemma swallowed uneasily and she felt like crying.

Suddenly, a tall, smiling boy opened Jemma's truck door.

Chapter 3
Visitors arrive

"Hello! Hello!" Koyobe was keen to try out the English greeting he had learnt.

"Hi," Jemma answered quietly.

She looked around. Her mum was busy talking and gesturing and smiling. No one except Tembo understood what she was saying, but Jemma could tell her mum had already won everyone over.

She realised that the tall, smiling boy was trying to tell her something.

"Koyobe," he said, pointing to his chest. "Koyobe."

Jemma nodded. *Maybe that's his name.* She felt shy. She looked away and, not for the first time, she wished she felt confident and outgoing like her mum.

"Jem!" Her mum called her over. Jemma stood next to her as a round of introductions took place. Jemma smiled shyly, and everyone smiled and nodded.

"Come on, Jem. Let's get set up!" Jemma trailed after her mum as she unpacked the truck.

After setting up their tent and eating the sandwiches they had made that morning, Jemma felt more settled.

It's quite beautiful, she thought. *I'd love to draw those spiky trees and the unusually shaped rocks.*

"Musa and the others are taking us hunting," Jemma's mum said as she organised her camera equipment. "They're getting food for our feast tonight. It'll be so interesting!"

Jemma didn't like the idea of a hunting trip, and it made her stomach churn. "I think I'll stay here and do some drawing."

Jemma's mum hesitated.

"I'll be here," said Tembo, sensing Jemma's mum's concern. "Jemma will be fine."

"Okay then. I know how much you love drawing. But promise me you will stay at the camp. No exploring."

She kissed Jemma on the forehead and rushed off.

Jemma got out her pencils and drawing pad. As she started to draw, she could feel herself relax. Soon, she was engrossed in her work.

Jemma was concentrating hard when she sensed someone watching her. She looked up. It was Koyobe and he was trying to ask Jemma if she wanted to take a look around with him.

But Jemma wasn't sure what his unfamiliar words and unusual hand gestures meant. She didn't want to upset him, so she shook her head to show she didn't understand.

Koyobe sighed and turned away, disappointed that Jemma wasn't interested. He'd been excited to show the visitors his home and his culture, and he felt deflated.

Maybe that's how Dad feels when I complain about doing things with him, like going hunting for honey, he thought.

Chapter 4

Jemma explores

Jemma busily worked on her sketch. She was pleased with how it was looking.

Twit twit tah-weee. Twit twit tah-weee.

A persistent bird interrupted her, and she turned towards the sound.

"That's a honeyguide bird," Tembo explained. "If you follow it, it will take you to a beehive. And inside the beehive is the most beautiful honey you've ever tasted!"

Jemma laughed. Surely, Tembo was joking. "How can a bird show someone where a beehive is?"

"It's true." Tembo was serious. "Koyobe and his dad can take you honey hunting tomorrow. Koyobe's father, Musa, is the best honey hunter I've ever seen, and he is teaching Koyobe to become a great honey hunter, too."

"I'd like that," Jemma said as she smiled. And she meant it!

"I'll organise it for you," said Tembo. "But for now, I might have a little rest. This hot sun is making me drowsy. Come and get me if you need anything."

"Sure, Tembo. Thanks," Jemma said, and her attention went back to her drawing.

Twit twit tah-weee. Twit twit tah-weee.

Jemma was interrupted again.

What do you want, bird?

Twit twit tah-weee. Twit twit tah-weee.

Jemma looked closely at the bird.

You're cute, aren't you, bird? Stay still and I'll sketch you.

But as Jemma looked down, the bird flew off.

Twit twit tah-weee. Twit twit tah-weee.

Jemma spied the bird in a thick baobab tree.

Okay. I'll come to you.

She looked back. Tembo, Koyobe and everyone else in the camp were resting during the midday heat, so she grabbed a pencil and her sketchpad, and followed the bird to the next tree. But just as she reached the bird, it flew off to another tree.

Jemma laughed. *Do you think this is a game, bird?*

Jemma quickened her pace to catch up with the bird. She stopped to begin her sketch, and again, the bird flew to another tree.

Not again! Stay still, bird! Jemma thought.

Jemma followed the noisy bird as it flitted from tree to tree.

Eventually, the bird landed on the branch of a tree, and this time, it stayed still. Jemma began her sketch. As she sketched, she suddenly felt a sharp sting on her hand.

"Ouch!" She let out a startled cry.

A bee had stung Jemma's hand and the sting hurt badly. She looked up and saw a beehive, with angry buzzing bees swarm around it. She panicked and turned to run, but as she did so, a long, sharp acacia spike ripped at her skin and drew blood.

"Ouch!" Jemma cried out again. She ran from the beehive, but as she did, her shoe slipped in the dust. She stumbled and fell. *Thud!*

"Owww!" Jemma rubbed her knee. She slowly got up and limped over to the closest tree.

Jemma looked at the deep cut on her arm and her swollen han

I've got to get back to the camp, she thought.

She looked around in every direction, but she could no longer see the camp. A wave of panic swept over Jemma. Everything looked the same and she had no idea which way to go!

She took some slow, deep breaths as she tried to block out the panic.

What should I do?

No one even knows I've left the camp.

And what if they can't find me?

Jemma crumpled to the ground as tears tumbled out of her eyes and rolled down her cheeks.

Chapter 5

A lucky meeting

Koyobe awoke from his nap. He stretched and yawned.

Twit twit tah-weee. Twit twit tah-weee.

"Don't hassle me, bird. I don't feel like going honey hunting."

Koyobe was feeling lazy, but the bird was persistent and continued to whistle, until Koyobe eventually gave in. He grabbed his axe and a fire stick. He whistled back to the bird, and headed off as it flew along.

Soon enough, the bird stopped. Koyobe looked up into the tree nearby. *There it is,* he thought. He was about to climb up when he heard an unfamiliar voice.

"Help me!"

Koyobe turned – *it was Jemma, the Australian girl!*

Koyobe raced over to her.

"Koyobe?" Jemma couldn't believe he was there. "I'm so happy to see you." And her tears flowed again.

When Koyobe saw Jemma's red, swollen hand, he grimaced. He got some sap from the tree trunk and gently rubbed it onto her hand. The sap immediately soothed the pain.

"Thank you." Jemma smiled at Koyobe through her tears.

Koyobe pointed over to the tree with the beehive as he motioned for Jemma to sit down on a rock. Jemma watched as Koyobe raced up the tree with his fire stick. He opened the beehive and stuck the smoking stick inside. He then sliced the hive wide open with his axe and pulled out large pieces of honeycomb.

Koyobe brought some to Jemma and gestured for her to try it. She put the rich, golden honeycomb in her mouth and sucked at the sweet, strong syrup.

"Yum!" She looked at Koyobe with big, wide eyes.

Koyobe was instantly proud, and glad that he had watched and learnt from his father.

Then they sat together in the shade, eating honeycomb.

After collecting the rest of the honeycomb, Koyobe and Jemma walked back to the camp. Koyobe pointed out different landforms, plants and animals they saw, and they chatted and giggled the whole way back. Jemma was surprised how well they understood each other, even though neither of them knew what the other one was actually saying.

As they got closer to the camp, Jemma grabbed Koyobe by the arm. She knew her mother would be annoyed if she found out that she had left the camp by herself and had to be rescued.

"Don't tell them I was lost. Please. Our secret?" Jemma put her finger to her lips.

"Yes! Yes!" Koyobe nodded as he, too, put his finger to his lips. "See – cret!" he said.

That night, the mood was festive and happy as everyone sat around the campfire and ate a delicious feast. A full moon lit up the night sky that was covered with a blanket of stars.

Jemma and Koyobe sat side by side and laughed as Tembo told funny stories about his exploits as a tour guide.

Jemma and her mum taught the Hadza people some English words. Koyobe's attempts had everyone in fits of laughter.

Tembo then interpreted for Jemma and her mum as Musa and some of the others told traditional Hadza tales.

The night ended with everyone singing Hadza songs as the fire reflected on their faces.

As Jemma took it all in, she felt a twinge of sadness. She was disappointed that she and her mum had to leave the next day. She would miss these amazing people. And she would miss her new friend Koyobe, the Hadza honey hunter.

Epilogue

Six months later

Koyobe stopped what he was doing as he heard the distant sound of a motor. He squinted through the dust and saw the shape of Tembo's truck.

Koyobe's face broke into a smile. It was always great to see Tembo.

"Look what I have!" Tembo shouted as he jumped out of his truck.

He waved a glossy magazine above his head. Musa, Koyobe and all the others crowded around to see.

"It's the article about you. Look!" Tembo opened the magazine. There were photos of them all. They pointed in awe and they felt a great sense of pride. Tembo read the article aloud before the magazine was passed around from person to person.

"And this is for you, Koyobe." Tembo handed Koyobe an envelope. "It's from Jemma," he added with a grin.

Koyobe ripped open the envelope. Inside was a drawing of him.

Koyobe couldn't believe how much it looked like him.

"What does this say, Tembo?" Koyobe pointed to Jemma's handwriting.

It read: *To my friend, Koyobe. Thanks for sharing your honey. Jemma.*

Koyobe smiled to himself as he looked at the drawing.

He would treasure it forever.

A note from the author

When I first heard about the Hadza people of Tanzania, I was amazed! The Hadza do not get stressed easily. They are calm and relaxed, and are never in a rush. I wanted this to be a message in my story.

It would be very interesting to visit the Hadza people, but there would also be difficult parts such as the language barrier. When I was developing the character of Jemma, I kept this in mind.

My story ended with Jemma and Koyobe becoming friends because, despite how different they were, they realised that they had lots in common, too.